CAREER AS A
FLORIST

FLORAL DESIGNER
FLOWER GROWER

WHO DOESN'T LOVE A BEAUTIFUL bouquet of flowers? It is hard to think of any occasion when flowers do not add a special touch. Even in the heart of winter, in the coldest regions of the world, the zesty crisp smell, stunning array of bright colors, and eclectic shapes and sizes of freshly cut flowers grouped in an imaginative arrangement perk up everyone's day and seem to warm the frosty air and melt the snow away.

Florists and flower growers spend their days amid nature's wonders and have the good fortune of being able to pass these horticultural treasures on to others. Flowers have a language of their own. Without words they can convey a variety of feelings and emotions, from love to good wishes.

Floral delights have become favored gifts for birthdays, anniversaries, Mother's Day, Valentine's Day, and various holidays. These attractive arrays of eye-popping petals, supported by flowing stems, are sent to congratulate people on job promotions, graduations, great performances, marvelous successes, and just about anything else where nothing but flowers can enhance the moment.

Adding to the thrill is the element of surprise, as many a bouquet arrives unexpectedly from a well-wisher in a far-off place, or simply around the corner. At proms, weddings, awards ceremonies, and retirement dinners, inspiring and breathtaking floral designs – precisely placed in decorative vases, perfectly positioned throughout a room – give a well-worn banquet hall new life and make it look different for every special event.

Working tirelessly behind the scenes are floral designers and flower growers. What starts out as a single seed can end up as a botanical spectacle, the likes of which people will not soon forget. Hours of painstaking work are put into these floral masterpieces. They spring from the efforts of people throughout the floral industry, whether they are in the field growing and harvesting flowers, in a studio planning and designing floral arrangements, or in a retail shop, helping customers select the ideal flowers for that once-in-a-lifetime moment.

This is a career that takes patience and talent. It also requires business savvy and marketing expertise. A retail flower shop can become a community stalwart, where you can build a reputation with your designs and creativity. You work with more than just flowers, as you incorporate balloons, bows, ribbons, stuffed animals, even fruit and other plant life into your creations. You know which colors work well together and can play off various themes in crafting floral arrangements that are both charming and distinctive.

As a flower grower, you can become known for the quality and variety of the flowers you produce. Working in both greenhouses and in the field, you use only the best seeds and soil, as well as the latest equipment to produce the finest flowers possible in this very competitive field. You are more than a flower grower, as you hone your skills, both in sales and distribution, to support your flower production efforts.

The best part of being in the floral industry are the smiles flowers bring to everyone's face.

WHAT YOU CAN DO NOW

LEARN AS MUCH AS YOU CAN ABOUT flowers and horticulture. Local flower clubs and societies are excellent sources of information, and by joining one, you might also find a mentor willing to teach you about flowers and their care.

Flower shows are held throughout the country. They spotlight floriculture, horticulture, and the floral industry, as well as gardening and landscaping. Exhibitors are more than happy to talk about all types of flowers and plant life. Many of these shows offer classes on floral design and display exhibits of outstanding examples of the craft. Some of the classes give you a chance to try your hand at floral design with an expert looking on offering suggestions. You will meet people who share your interest and are knowledgeable about all aspects of the floral industry.

State and county fairs around the United States feature exhibits of flowers and plants common to their particular regions. There is always plenty of information available about the featured flowers and plants, with tips about growing and caring for them. Flower growers and floral designers attend and exhibit at these fairs, making them an ideal learning ground for someone who wants to get into the floral business.

If you live near a botanical garden, visit the facility often. Spend some time studying the exhibits and the write-ups that accompany them. Consider volunteering at the facility to get some hands-on experience working with flowers, plants, and gardens.

HISTORY OF THE CAREER

SINCE THE EARLIEST CIVILIZATIONS, flowers have enriched lives and held symbolic meaning. For instance, azaleas represent abundance; lilacs, first love; calla lilies, royalty; orchids, delicate beauty; statice, success; irises, inspiration; and on and on. Almost any emotion can be conveyed through flowers, even warnings. If you get rhododendrons, someone is telling you to beware.

The beauty of flowers has always captured the eye and dazzled the senses. Ancient Egyptians almost five thousand years ago, lavishly decorated with flowers nourished by the Nile. They made wreaths and garlands by weaving flowers and foliage together with brightly colored fruit. The Nile Valley was home to roses, irises, lilies, narcissus, and a variety of other blue, yellow, and red blooming specimens. The flowers were harvested and put in baskets, vases, and bowls to be given as gifts or to adorn dinner tables.

The Greeks and Romans of ancient times were influenced by the Egyptians, and not only used flowers for decorative enhancement but also valued them for their fragrance. They wore floral garlands around their necks, and leafy, flower-laden wreaths on their heads. They employed professionals to make these festive floral arrangements.

These cultures used flowers to honor gods and heroes. The winners of ancient Olympic competitions were presented with laurel wreaths, as were winners of poetry contests and those who excelled in military battles. The Greeks meticulously arranged flowers in upright cornucopias (horns of plenty), delivering the finished products as gifts.

Flower arrangements were seen everywhere in Europe by 1000 AD. People began seeking out talented individuals with the ability to create special floral designs. By the 1700s, flowers began to take on a new role. British men and woman carried fragrant nosegays – small handheld bouquets – everywhere they went to combat noxious odors in the air.

Floral design came of age in the Victorian Era of the 19th century. This was a time of peace, prosperity, and refinement in the British Empire during the reign of Queen Victoria. Many traditional techniques and design styles used in modern-day floral arrangements were formulated during this period. Most of these would be considered too elaborate today, but others have been adapted and are still mainstays of floral design. By 1900 floral design was recognized as a true vocation, and the trade was taught to students.

Meanwhile, the elements of floral design in England were crossing the Atlantic to the United States. Upper-class society showed off their affluence by having huge, excessive, even gaudy floral arrangements made for display in their homes. The White House started using fresh flowers in the 1850s, replacing the wax ones popular at the time. The change to fresh flowers came at the suggestion of President James Buchanan's niece, Harriet Lane, who saw live flower arrangements in government buildings all over England when she toured that nation. Lane acted as first lady during her uncle's presidency (1857-1861) because he was a lifelong bachelor.

As flower shops began to proliferate in the United States in the late 1800s, a group of florists, nurserymen, and seedsmen (plant and flower growers) got together at a floricultural trade show in Chicago in 1884. The result was the establishment of the Society of American Florists and the beginning of an effort to promote the florist profession.

By the end of the 19th century, England was pioneering another floral industry innovation – growing flowers commercially on a large scale. Flower growers grew their crops on large estates and then harvested the flowers for sale to retailers throughout that nation. In the US, farmers allotted at least part of their fields to growing a variety of flowers and plants destined for retail sale.

The next big advance in the industry came on August 18, 1910, in Rochester, New York. A group of 15 florists got together and formed the Florists' Telegraph Delivery Association (FTD). A flower-by-wire cooperative, this group allowed its members to exchange orders for out-of-town delivery. The exchange was done by telegraph. Before FTD, individual florists shipped flowers either by train or by mail to out-of-town recipients. FTD created standard bouquets so customers knew the arrangement they saw in one shop would be the same as the one created by a member shop in another locale.

Following World War I, Americans got involved in more peaceful pursuits, and a number of garden and flower clubs were started. This gave a boost to the flower industry. The industry enjoyed another boon after World War II in 1945, when exotic flowers were exported from foreign countries to the United States and found their way into floral designs.

As the environmental movement took hold in the 1970s and '80s, flowers and plants staged yet another resurgence as natural decor for homes and offices became symbols of green living.

THE WORK YOU WILL DO

FLORAL DESIGNERS AND FLOWER growers help make the world a more beautiful place. They only have a narrow window of time in which to perform their magic, because the product they work with is perishable. That one concept – the short life span of a flower once it is fully grown, harvested, and sent to market – guides much of the industry.

Because of how fragile flowers are, as soon as they are brought in from the field, the clock starts ticking on how long they will be a viable, saleable product. That makes the flower grower and the floral designer a team racing against time to get the flowers to the consumer and make a profit on the sale. Who knew that something so beautiful and delicate could create such pressure? So the mission becomes quite clear: have everything ready to go so nothing gets in the way of selling those flowers.

Florist
Floral Designer

To succeed in the flower industry, you have to be an excellent planner. Although the work may be fast-paced and demanding in a flower shop, as the shop owner, you have to do everything possible to keep it from becoming disorganized. That means being able to plan every day's work in advance, including time to fit in the unexpected, so that everything is handled and finished efficiently. That is how you succeed in this business, and how you make money.

A shop owner or manager must develop an overall plan for the daily operation of the shop, and the floral designers employed there must have a plan to get their work done. You need an open line of communications with everyone involved.

During busy seasons, such as the week before Valentine's Day and Mother's Day, or during months when you have many weddings scheduled, all the employees must know what their assignments are. You go over the list of flowers and supplies that are needed. Everything has to be on hand when it comes time to do a job. Being unprepared wastes time and costs money.

Employees must be aware that they might be called on to put in some overtime, and if they are not available, they have to inform you far enough in advance so you can make other arrangements. You can always step in yourself and help with the work.

You pay particular attention to ordering. You have to know your clientele – what they like and what they buy. Being aware of how sales went in past years during similar holidays and busy periods is essential. Record-keeping skills are important to help you make prudent decisions. You need to be very careful when ordering flowers and plants because of the perishable nature of the merchandise.

You devise clever new ways to get a sales advantage, like sending emails to your regular customers – and prospective ones as well – around major holidays like Valentine's Day and Christmas, urging them to order early to get the freshest flower arrangements possible. Those early orders can give you an indication of how many flowers and how much plant material you will likely need to handle the rush. You also have to come up with ideas to quickly move leftover flowers once the crush has passed, so as little as possible is wasted.

Some years weather conditions are optimal, so there is a glut of certain flowers on the market, making them inexpensive. Other years, Mother Nature lets you down and the flowers you need are in high demand and short supply. You have to be able to improvise.

You praise your staff when they come through during a particularly busy time. After all, to meet these extremely tight deadlines everybody has to help carry the load. Employees need to know you appreciate their efforts every time they do a good job. Hiring employees – and firing them, if necessary – are the flower shop owner's responsibility.

Pricing is an important job you have. In addition, you will be the one deciding if the store will sell other types of goods, like dried flowers, balloons, baskets, and related items. You also choose what types of plants, including dish gardens, will be sold in the shop.

Networking will help your shop get orders during slow times. As the owner, you meet with those in charge of other establishments, like catering halls, funeral homes, restaurants, hotels, and houses of worship, so they become familiar with your work and will refer clients your way if people ask for a recommendation.

When it comes to planning major events for customers, the flower shop owner and one of the other floral designers generally sit down with clients to discuss what is needed. This is where both you and the designers play many different roles. You are the experts, the creative talent, and also advisors, confidants, planners, salespeople, and very good listeners. Your goal is to have this special day go exactly the way the customers expect. When customers look back at pictures from the event, you want them to say the flowers were just exquisite.

You pay careful attention to what clients want, you tweak it a bit, make some suggestions, show them some photos of what works. Sometimes customers are so excited about an event, especially a wedding, they tend to go overboard. It is your job to gently and tactfully get their feet back on the ground and convince them of a plan that will get them exactly what will make them happy, for a price they can afford.

For big events like weddings, florists will go on site and place each flower arrangement exactly where they feel it belongs. Placement is very important. Some flower arrangements are too big or too small for certain spots. They look out of place and everyone can tell.

Floral designers who do not own their own shop have more time to do what they really love, to fashion flowers into wondrous displays of natural beauty. Floral designers must keep working at their craft, learning new styles and techniques. You have to experiment, adding your own personal touch to the latest popular styles.

You can never lose sight of the fundamentals. Each design used for an event has to stand on its own, yet fit into the overall theme. Colors have to work together. There has to be an easy flow and rhythm to each design.

All your pieces must incorporate the basic principles of floral design – balance, proportion, unity, and harmony. A floral designer looks at a single flower differently. You see how that flower can fit into the bigger picture. Every design starts out with a single flower. Some floral designers sketch out a piece before they make it. That gives them a chance to visualize it and refine it before putting in the work and using the flowers to make it.

To stay within budget and complete a project as planned, floral designers have to perfect the skill of estimating the number of flowers that will be needed for a wedding, an engagement party, or an anniversary or retirement dinner. Some of these designers will use any left over flowers to make a few extra arrangements, just in case they see a bare spot once they put out all the flower arrangements the customer ordered.

Floral designers also create pieces for sale in the shop. Flowers are not just about special orders. People often come in and buy something, an arrangement, plant, or simple cut flowers, off the shelf or from the cooler. Shops generally have a dozen or more floral arrangements on display every day.

Dyeing flowers is another aspect of this job. Sometimes, as on St. Patrick's Day, you need green carnations; for Halloween, you might want black ones to go with orange lilies.

Flower Growers

Florists and floral designers rely on flower growers. To run a flower-growing operation you need to be a strong decision maker with a solid background in agriculture and management. It is crucial for you to know what your land is capable of producing and the best floral crops to grow. One of the first decisions you make every growing season is which crops you are going to plant and how much acreage you are going to devote to each type of flower. Flower growers have to know their market and what their clients want. Since your customer base consists of wholesalers and distributors, you have to understand what their customers need and want as well.

You try to grow a variety of flowers so wholesalers and distributors can get everything they need from your farm without having to shop around. This is convenient for them and a smart business practice for you.

Overseeing soil preparation and keeping a watchful eye on the crops from seeds to grown flowers are part of your job. Pruning, spraying, fertilizing, and watering crops are regular duties. Inspecting the crops is something you do often. Keeping machinery up and running helps cut down on lost time.

Part of your education as a flower grower revolves around identifying and combating the diseases and insects that threaten your crops. Knowing about the climate and weather conditions in your area keeps you prepared to meet the challenges Mother Nature throws your way. You also need to be aware of all health and safety regulations related to agriculture.

Harvesting and packaging the flowers for shipment are the next steps. Included in this process is grading the flowers, so buyers know exactly what they are getting.

Managers in the flower-growing field hire and train employees. They also stay on top of the innovative trends in flower growing and the flower industry, like growing organic flowers. Many flower growers split their time between being out in the field and working in a greenhouse. They have to know how to care for flowers and plants growing in each of those environments, and in every season.

When they are not busy supervising the actual flower-growing operation, owners and managers are trying to develop more business. This requires meeting with wholesalers, distributors, and even retailers. Some retailers buy their flowers directly from the farms that grow them.

Most flower growers spend at least some of their time doing the hands-on work of planting and harvesting the flowers.

STORIES OF PEOPLE IN THE CAREER

I Am a Freelance Floral Designer

"I got into floral design for two reasons. First, I find working with flowers very relaxing. Second, I wanted to make floral arrangements for family events like barbecues and Thanksgiving dinner.

I got a bit carried away and made quite a few floral arrangements for these events. Then several family members asked me if I would mind making flower arrangements for their weddings. Several of the guests at these weddings asked me if I would do the flowers for their weddings. Before I knew it I had a nice little business going.

I work out of my home. I like working freelance because I only take the jobs I really want. There is no pressure to have to meet rent or other expenses that come with running a business out of a storefront.

Mine is really a niche business because I primarily focus on one type of event – weddings. I've learned a lot as I have gone along. I took several floral design courses and each one gave me new insights. Each of the instructors has a unique approach. Learning from a variety of people gives you different views of floral design – not just the art form, but also the business, the flowers to use, the base material, the best tools, and even shortcuts to getting the job done when you're swamped with orders.

When you start getting paid to make floral designs for other people's events, the work is a bit different than creating something for your own or your friend's pleasure. For instance, every bride has a favorite flower. You have to know where to get that flower, in quantity, if you can at that time of year. If you can't get it, you have to be able to suggest a suitable alternative. You can't just make a substitution of your own choosing. That means knowing about flowers that look very similar to the one the bride wants that might fit the bill. The essence of the job is keeping everyone happy. Once you have that special favorite flower, you want to create a design that makes it stand out.

In general, in this work you have to know which types of flowers are available during various times of the year and what colors they come in. You need to know which flowers will stay the freshest sitting in vases for hours and how to care for them. It's not necessary to take courses in floriculture, but I found some basic classes offered in community colleges near me. I would also recommend reading as much as you can about various flowers. You should know as much about them as possible. Clients ask questions and you have to have the answers.

For me this is not just a job. I love being around flowers and working with them. This started out as a hobby for me and I'm very proud of how it's grown into a real business. Not everyone can make money doing something they love. I think you really have to love flowers to be successful at floral design. I think it takes a passion and that shows in your designs."

I Own a Retail Flower Shop

"My flower shop is located in a vibrant business district in a suburban town. We are located near a train station and a bus stop. We get a great deal of walk-in business, as well as a substantial number of phone and Internet orders.

This is the only flower shop in town, but there are shops located in the nearby communities so we are not without competition. This is a fairly wealthy town, so it provides us with a good client base.

I think my shop does better than the average flower shop because people in this town have a lot of parties and usually order flowers for these events. We also get a lot of weddings, Bar Mitzvahs, and corporate banquets. The people in this town really love flowers and some people come by every week just to buy fresh flowers, plants, and floral arrangements to have in their homes.

To me, customer service is the most important thing about running a business like this. People don't have to come in here. If they feel you will go the extra mile for them and are happy to do it, they will keep coming back. I think we do well because we get a good amount of repeat business, and I think customer service has a great deal to do with that.

Everybody who works here loves flowers and I think that comes through. We all know our plants and flowers. We can talk to people about them, give them some interesting trivia about flowers, and tell them how to care for what they take home. We take time with our customers and we genuinely like our customers. We haven't lost that personal touch, and I won't allow that to happen. I think people look forward to coming in here. They have a good experience, leave with a good feeling. It all adds up to making this a successful enterprise.

Knowing your client base well gives you a chance to order the flowers they like so you have what they want when they come into the shop. Flowers are perishable, so ordering properly cuts down on waste and saves us money. There's a knack to ordering properly. It's something you pick up over time and it's essential for you to learn how to do it.

I'm a floral designer and I like to do some of the floral arrangements myself. I don't ever want to stop doing that, but I employ three other floral designers because we get pretty busy, and I have to take care of many necessary business matters. I can't devote as much time to making floral designs as I would like, and to me that is a bit of a drawback in owning my own store.

We like to make our floral designs special. There are a lot of floral designers out there, so you want to make your work stand out. The flowers, the form, the way the colors work together, the vases, the whole look – you want it to catch people's eye. You want people talking about the flowers. You want to wow them – after all, you get into this business to do something extraordinary. This is our stage, our time to shine. I figure, let's make the most of it."

I Am a Flower Grower

"First and foremost, I am a farmer. A lot of people don't realize that flower growers are farmers. I have other crops – fruits and vegetables – besides flowers. I know there are flower growers who use their land strictly for flowers, but from a business standpoint I think it's best to diversify. My family has farmed this land for generations and we always grew fruit, vegetables, and flowers. The different crops have kept us in business all these years. You can't rely on one type of crop. Farming is a risky business as it is. If you gamble on just a few crops, maybe one in particular, you can easily lose the farm.

I also have several greenhouses on the property where we grow plants all year round and some flowers off-season. We grow a variety of flowers. This was a business decision. We want to give our customers, flower distributors, as many choices as we can and keep them from having to shop around to get the mix of flowers they need to satisfy their customers.

We have been pretty successful with our flowers, and despite all the pitfalls out there have never suffered a loss on our crops. The fact that we also have a wide variety of fruits and vegetables helps us sell our flowers, even though, like everyone else in this business in the United States, we have to fend off cheap imports. I feel our flowers last longer than the imports because we can get them to market faster and into the hands of the end customer. I'm proud of our products and how long they last once they get to market. I think people will spend a little more for a good product.

We mostly sell to wholesalers and distributors, but we have our own small store on the property and we also sell at fruit and farmer's markets. That gives us a chance to meet people and hear what they are thinking. Customers know who they are buying from, and when they are happy with what they bought, they will come back and buy from you again.

I guess people don't think about it much, but when they do buy flowers locally and they look fresher right from the get-go and last longer overall, they say, 'Wow! How come?' Then you explain to them that they come from around the corner and don't have to make it through a long plane trip from a foreign country, a truck ride to market, and then a trip to the store. All the middlemen are cut out, and the flowers come fresh from the field to you.

You have got to educate the public about what they are

buying, the quality, and why it costs a bit more. We use the best of everything when we grow our crops. We are your neighbors. You know our name. We put our reputation on the line with every flower and piece of fruit we sell.

We are dedicated to providing quality, and that takes hard work. Our flowers and plants are our marketing tools and we want them to be the best for people who want to buy the best. We feel that way about our fruits and vegetables, too. This is a competitive business and whether you are out in field all day long, including many weekends, or split your time between office work, the store, and the field, you come home dirty and tired every night. It's a good feeling."

PERSONAL QUALIFICATIONS

FIRST, YOU REALLY MUST LOVE FLOWERS. That is the number-one requirement for floral designers, flower growers, and anyone in the flower industry. You will be surrounded by flowers all day, so if your passion begins to wane, it could put your career in jeopardy.

Floral designers must be artistic, creative, and bursting with ideas. Those ideas must be bold, fresh, and inventive, and you have to be able to turn them into color-coordinated, well-balanced, and stylish floral arrangements.

Customers need to see you as enthusiastic and confident. They come to you to be inspired by your plan for floral designs to make their special event extraordinary. You are cool under fire, handle pressure with ease, and are a skillful problem solver.

Organization is one of your key traits. Everything has its place, and there is an order to the way work is done. Floral designers have an eye for detail. They can draw on the theme of an event, and incorporate it into floral designs that make an occasion memorable.

This field calls for keeping up with the times, knowing about new styles, following the current trends, recognizing the flowers that are popular at the moment, and staying on top of the latest innovations in the field.

A high level of manual dexterity is also essential for floral designers. You need to gently manipulate flowers to look their best.

Understanding people is crucial. You have to take what customers tell you and mold it into your floral arrangements. Excellent communications skills – both with customers and with employees – are necessary on this job.

Flexibility is important, too. It allows you to make substitutions and keep a project going without missing a beat.

Floral designers and flower growers who operate businesses have to be strong managers. They must be able to motivate employees, recognize talent, and use their administrative skills.

Careers in the flower industry require a certain amount of patience. When you are working with nature, things do not always go according to plan. Factors beyond your control – the weather, for instance – may cause delays, but with a bit of persistence you can get back on track. Patience also helps florists deal with edgy brides and nervous prom dates. It gives flower growers the ability to cope with demanding and finicky wholesalers and distributors.

Flower growers are farmers, so to pursue this career you must have a strong affinity for agriculture. When you are in the flower business, you have to be knowledgeable. People are going to ask your advice about caring for plants and flowers. They consider you an expert, and if you give them solid, dependable information, you will have a loyal customer for a long time.

Are you allergic to pollen or any kind of foliage? That could make working in the flower industry highly uncomfortable.

ATTRACTIVE FEATURES

SOME FLOWER SHOP OWNERS SET aside time each day to make deliveries. They have someone on staff who could do that job, but they would rather do it themselves and see the smiles, surprise, and delight of people who do not expect to be getting flowers.

Few occupations can offer such satisfaction every single day. In a world that technology makes more impersonal all the time, what could be better than ringing a doorbell, handing someone a bouquet of flowers, and watching the reaction as you make that person's day special?

Customers coming into a flower shop are filled with unbridled enthusiasm. They cannot wait to see your creations, or tell you what they want and see you express their emotions through your designs. Your customers are mesmerized by how you manipulate each flower into just the right position in a floral arrangement just for you.

Floral design tests your skills and your creativity. When you are not crafting a floral arrangement for someone else, you are free to see where your imagination takes you as you create designs for display in your shop.

This is a people-oriented business. You are not just sitting at a desk looking at a computer screen all day. People get flowers and plants to liven up the atmosphere in their home and workplace, to keep the mood happy and upbeat. You already have this pleasant environment all around you throughout the workday, setting a positive tone in a colorful, nature-filled, clean environment. You are always on the move and the work never gets dull. There are no business suits required in this casual setting; blue jeans will do just fine.

Helping people is part of the job. When people are having a special event, they know they want flowers but usually they do not know exactly what kind. You can guide them through the decision-making process so that it is not only painless but also fun.

Inevitably, a florist will have to supply flowers for a funeral and, in this case, you can help lift the burden from the grieving family by taking over the task and providing precisely what is needed in a timely fashion.

One of the best aspects of working in the flower industry is that it does not take years of formal education to learn the basics of floral design or flower growing. Starting out in this new career, you are ready to see what you can do. As you grow in the business, you refine your skills, develop your philosophy, define your vision, hone your talent, and crystallize your approach. You grow with the job.

When you work with flowers and plants, you are surrounded by beauty. Flower growers can see it acre after acre. Floral designers have it at their fingertips. They harvest that beauty or capture it in a floral arrangement and pass it along to other people.

UNATTRACTIVE FEATURES

JOBS IN THE FLOWER INDUSTRY ARE hard work and can be physically demanding. Floral designers have to lift heavy buckets of flowers and spend most of the day on their feet.

During busy times of the year, like Mother's Day and Valentine's Day, florists put in long hours day after day. The same is true if you have a series of weddings back to back.

Flower shops are often open in the evening and on weekends, so you probably will not be able to take a day off when everyone else does, and you will work on many holidays as well.

Flower growers do constant bending, working on their hands and knees in the soil in a hot field. The work can wreak havoc on the hands of both designers and growers, and can make them rough and sore.

Naturally, weather conditions vary and flower growers often work out in the rain. Greenhouses are hot and uncomfortable for those who have to stay in them for long periods. Floral designers may have to spend some time in refrigerated coolers working with flowers. In addition, there is a risk of injury – florists and growers use sharp tools.

The flower industry is a seasonal business. Prime seasons and big holidays can be very hectic, with constant pressure to get all the work done. It can become overwhelming, but you do not want to turn down any work because those sales will help you make it through the dry spells.

No matter how frantic things get, you must stay calm to set the proper tone for your staff. Customer service has to remain top-notch even during these busy times. Many people judge you on how you handle things when the pressure is on.

Floral designers are creative people and do not enjoy dealing with the business end of things. If you own your own shop, you have to address these business issues. You have to order flowers and supplies. You have to process employee issues like payroll and taxes. You may struggle to find and keep good employees, and occasionally have to let someone go.

The flower-growing business is very competitive, not so much from US growers but from foreign growers who may flood the market with low-priced flowers they can produce inexpensively by hiring cheap labor. So keeping costs down is essential.

Unlike fruit, flowers have to be aesthetically pleasing. They sell based on their good looks – no blotches, discolorations, flaws, faults, or marks. Any imperfections and you cannot sell the flower. That makes the work stressful especially since it involves factors not under your control, like weather conditions. A heavy rain, a sudden dip in temperatures, or a swift wind might leave you with some costly damage.

As a flower grower, you will probably cultivate several different types of flowers to ensure that at least some of your crops will be successful and you will make a profit. Each crop of flowers requires special care. Making sure each crop gets what it needs can be painstaking, time-consuming work.

EDUCATION AND TRAINING

YOU CAN TAKE ANY OF SEVERAL DIFFRERENT approaches to training for this career. Graduating from high school is the first step.

Some formal education in floral design or flower growing is not generally required, but it enhances your chances of getting into the flower industry. Without it, you will have to rely on an experienced florist or flower grower willing to hire you without much experience and then spend the time and effort to train you. Those opportunities are hard to find.

There are many floral design schools around the country. Most major cities have at least one. Take the time to explore the various curricula offered at these schools and see what is best for you.

The Palmer School of Floral Design in Fort Collins, Colorado, for example, has a floral design certification program consisting of a series of four courses, each requiring 25 hours of instruction. The classes are small and start at beginner level, working all the way through an advanced level. Students get hands-on experience making everything from corsages and boutonnieres with basic designs, to more complicated wedding bouquets and topiaries.

Founded in 1969, the Floral Design Institute in Portland, Oregon, has hundreds of courses in creating floral arrangements, from simple two-hour classes to a series of extensive certification programs. The school has received nationwide recognition for its diverse curriculum. Students can receive a basic floral design certificate after completing a 120-hour course of study at the school and passing both a written and a design exam. Classes in the three-- week course teach students how to make floral arrangements for all special occasions, and what needs to be included in designs for events like engagement parties and weddings, as well as holidays such as Valentine's Day and Mother's Day. Certificates are also available in advanced floral design and wedding floral specialist. In addition, the school has classes in business for floral entrepreneurs.

Many community colleges, like Harford Community College in Maryland and El Paso Community College in Texas offer certificates in floral design through their continuing education departments. The requirements to get a certificate, including how many classes you have to take, vary from school to school.

Kishwaukee College in Illinois, awards a two-year associate degree in applied science in floral design. Courses include floral marketing, flower store management, and wedding and corsage design. The school also offers a two-year associate degree in applied science in horticulture – the science of growing flowers, fruits, and vegetables – which is an alternative path for floral designers and a good course of study for flower growers.

A two-year associate in applied science degree in floral design and interior plantscape management is available at Joliet Junior College in Illinois. A wide range of coursework includes basic floral design, dried and silk flower design, wedding and sympathy designs, and party and event work. The associate degree program includes 19 weeks of work experience. The school has a one-year certificate program in floral design as well, which is not as extensive as the two-year degree program.

A number of other colleges around the country offer similar two-year associate degree programs in floral design and horticulture.

There are also four-year college degrees. In the Department of Plant and Soil Sciences at Mississippi State University, students can earn a Bachelor of Science degree in horticulture with a floral management concentration, a floriculture and ornamental horticulture concentration, or a fruit and vegetable production concentration. A four-year degree might seem like too much education for those who want to get right out into the workforce. You can always take a closer look at these types of programs later on if you want to further your education or enhance your credentials.

State floral associations, like the Texas State Florists' Association and the Michigan Floral Association, have regular floral design classes for those looking to get into the field. Other floral associations, including the Louisiana State Florists' Association, team up with colleges in their states to offer courses, including beginning and continuing education classes. Louisiana is the only state that requires florists to be licensed.

You can also take online courses in floral design or flower growing. A good selection of these is offered at online colleges like Penn Foster Career School and Ashworth College.

The American Institute of Floral Designers has a well-respected certification program for floral designers with rigorous requirements that must be met by all applicants. Some state floral associations, including the California State Floral Association, offer certifications to florists and floral designers in their states. These certifications are not required, but they are helpful in getting a job or impressing potential clients.

EARNINGS

MANY VARIABLES AFFECT THE INCOME of floral designers and flower growers. For designers, it often depends on where a flower shop is located. Shops with a larger customer base in more affluent areas do more in sales and yield better incomes for owners and employees.

Floral designers employed by flower shops usually get paid about $20 an hour, based on experience. That adds up to an annual salary of about $40,000 full time.

Floral designers can supplement their income by teaching floral-design classes. However, getting hired for a teaching job requires extensive on-the-job experience and an impressive résumé.

Once you have that, you can also get paid to do floral-design workshops at flower shows.

For floral designers, the most money comes from owning a shop. Being a shop owner means less time for floral design and more time spent running the business. Most flower shop owners earn between 10 and 15 percent of their total sales. A shop with $500,000 in annual sales will yield an income of $50,000 to $75,000 for its owner.

There is no limit on how much you can do in sales. Real go-getters can increase sales – and their income – substantially. Some flower shops sell other items, like small gifts, vases, stuffed animals, and greeting cards. Others also make up and deliver fruit baskets.

Beginning flower growers are usually hourly wage earners, in the $10 to $15 range, amounting to a yearly salary of roughly $20,000 to $35,000 full time. Managers can earn in the $60,000 range.

The real money in this end of the business is in owning a flower-growing operation. Most flower growers not only grow and sell flowers and plants, but fruits and vegetables as well. This can boost sales and increase income substantially. Salary for owners relates to sales, and take-home pay is 10 to 15 percent of annual business. Your income can be increased by running a small fruit and flower shop on the land where the fruits, vegetables, and flowers are grown, and selling directly to the public at open-air markets.

OPPORTUNITIES

INNOVATIVE FLORAL DESIGNERS WITH groundbreaking ideas are always in demand. As you develop a distinctive style, you help keep the field fresh and exciting, and that style sets you apart from other floral designers. You get better with each arrangement you create and you gain more confidence in your talents.

Wherever flowers are grown, someone is needed to display those flowers properly and shape them into stunning, unforgettable arrangements. If there is an area without a local florist, it is up to you to fill the void.

New ways of selling flowers to the public – at the supermarket, for instance – are coming to the fore all the time. That translates into more jobs in the flower industry.

Marketing yourself is a big part of creating opportunities in this field. Take pictures of your designs so you can show them to people interested in hiring you, either as a full-time employee or a freelancer.

Get your work seen. This may mean doing some free floral designs for local libraries, museums, or nursing homes in exchange for a sign giving you credit for the arrangement and putting your name out in the public.

Keep in mind that flower shops are only one way of succeeding in this field. Some floral designers work with flower wholesalers, making floral arrangements that are sold at convenience stores. Others develop ongoing relationships with interior designers and present their work in elegant homes and sprawling corporate headquarters. Resorts often house greenhouses and flower growing beds, and employ designers to decorate their lobbies and lounges with a constant flow of fresh blooms. Craft stores hire floral designers to teach classes on flower arranging, and to make floral arrangements using dried and artificial flowers for sale in the store.

Networking is very important in the floral industry. It opens up a host of opportunities in the field. People in the business want to know you are out there. They are always looking for new talent.

Most networking is done through national trade shows and floral associations, like the American Institute of Floral Designers. There are statewide trade associations, including the California State Floral Association and the Michigan Floral Association, throughout the United States.

Flower growers also have professional associations, such as the Association of Specialty Cut Flower Growers. Recently, flower growers in the United States have been getting a boost from a nationwide effort to encourage people to buy fruit, vegetables, and flowers from local growers.

The United States signed free-trade agreements with several South American countries in 1991. As a result, the nation was flooded with cheap floral imports, especially from Colombia, and that hurt flower growers in the United States. The cut-flower lobby has been fighting back, launching a campaign to get people to ask where the flowers they are buying are from and urging them to buy only homegrown flowers.

In 2013, the US Department of Agriculture started a program called Know Your Farmer, Know Your Flowers, which helped prompt the White House to begin using flowers grown in the United States for its state dinners. The effort to encourage people throughout the country to buy flowers grown in the United States is creating more job opportunities for the nation's flower growers and expanding the industry.

GETTING STARTED

WHETHER YOU ARE LOOKING FOR A career in floral design or flower growing, the best way to start in the flower industry is by working for someone else. In this business, experience counts. So learn as much as you can while you are in school and then get some hands--on experience.

In the flower industry, it is not hard to find someone willing to be your mentor. Most people in the flower business had a mentor when they started out and are more than happy to return the favor. Simply put, when it comes to selling or growing flowers, there are some lessons you have to learn on the job, like how to order supplies and how to quote prices.

Try to find a mentor who has been in the flower industry for a long time and knows how to deal with matters like rising costs, keeping the doors open during slow seasons, hiring and firing employees, providing customer service, and marketing. Successful florists know which flowers and plants are most profitable and sell the fastest in your area. Without hesitation, they know who to contact if they get a big order unexpectedly and need materials and supplies quickly. They can show you how to get the job done fast, without sacrificing quality, and still maximize profits.

Experienced flower growers will be able to share their knowledge about cultivating various flowers and foliage, and in what quantities. They can give you insight into the advantages and disadvantages of growing both indoors and outdoors. You will pick up flower-grading skills and learn about hydroponics – the art of growing plants in gravel, liquid, or sand. Most important, you will learn what works and what does not in this industry. Whether you start out as an intern, an apprentice, or an employee, you are gaining valuable experience that will serve you later in your career.

Many floral designers have acquired their own shops by working for someone else. The florist decides to leave the industry or retire, and offers to sell the shop to the floral designer who has been working there. You know the areas and the clientele, and the business is already established. It is an easy transition and a good way to take ownership of a flower shop.

If this opportunity does not come your way, you may still want to be in business for yourself. There are advantages to owning your own business, but perhaps you do not have access to the money to cover start-up costs. Many floral designers have reduced the cost of going into business by starting out in their own garage, rather than renting a storefront. You might have to bring in some refrigeration for the flowers, but you avoid a costly long-term lease. Then you can concentrate on marketing and building up your clientele.

Start by doing flower arrangements for family and friends' parties, weddings, and other special events. Once you have completed some jobs and have letters of recommendation, it is time to expand.

Contact the managers of hotels and catering facilities in your area and see if they need a floral designer. Send photos of your best floral arrangements so they can see your work up close, and include a note asking for a meeting. You might even send an actual arrangement you have done that shows your best work. Remember: everyone loves receiving flowers!

ASSOCIATIONS

■ **Society of American Florists (SAF)**

http://www.safnow.org

■ **National Alliance of Floral Associations (NAFA)**

www.aboutnafa.org/index.html

■ **Creative Floral Arrangers of the Americas (CFAA)**

http://cfaofa.org/links.html

■ **Independent Florists' Association (IFA)**

http://www.myifa.org/index

■ **American Institute of Floral Designers (AIFD)**

http://aifd.org

■ **Wholesale Florist & Florist Supplier Association (WFFSA)**

www.wffsa.org/aws/WFFSA/pt/sp/home_page

■ **Association of Specialty Cut Flower Growers**

http://www.ascfg.org

■ **AmericanHort**

http://americanhort.org

■ **Master Florists Association**

www.masterfloristsassn.org

■ **Hometown Florists Association**

www.hometownfloristsassociation.com/association

PERIODICALS

Florists' Review Magazine

Floral Design Magazine

The Flower Arranger

Fusion Flowers

Canadian Florist

Professional Florist

Floral Business

Floral Management Magazine

Flower Magazine

Wedding Flowers

Grower News

Greenhouse Grower

Greenhouse Management

Growing for Market

The Cut Flower Quarterly

WEBSITES

■ **American Rose Society**
http://www.ars.org

■ **American Orchid Society**
www.aos.org

■ **Plantscape Industry Alliance**
http://www.cipaweb.org

■ **World Flower Council**
http://www.worldflowercouncil.org

■ **American Horticultural Society**
http://www.ahs.org

■ **The Florist Guide**
http://www.thefloristguide.com\

■ **Massachusetts Flower Growers' Association**
www.massflowergrowers.com

■ **Florint: International Florist Organization**
http://www.florint.org

■ **The Florist Detectives**
http://floristdetective.com

SCHOOLS

■ **LISTING OF FLORAL DESIGN SCHOOLS**
http://www.thefloristguide.com/listings/category/usa

■ **Palmer School of Floral Design**
http://palmerschooloffloraldesign.com/index.htm

■ **Floral Design Institute**
www.floraldesigninstitute.com

■ **Harford Community College**
www.harford.edu/continuing-education.aspx

■ **El Paso Community College**
www.epcc.edu/ContinuingEd
/IndustryProfessionalTraining/Pages/ProfessionalFloralDe
signCertificate.aspx

■ **Kishwaukee College**
www.kishwaukeecollege.edu
/programs_of_study/pdf/HORT-Floral.pdf

■ **Joliet Junior College**
www.jjc.edu/academics/divisions/career-technical
/agriculture-horticulture/hort/Pages/floral-design
-info.aspx

■ **Mississippi State University**
http://www.pss.msstate.edu/students/floriculture.asp

■ **Penn Foster Career School**
http://www.pennfoster.edu/programs
-and-degrees/home-and-garden/floral
-design-career-diploma

■ **Ashworth College**
www.ashworthcollege.edu/career
-diplomas/floral-design

■ **Texas State Florists' Association**
http://www.tsfa.org/education.html

■ **Michigan Floral Association**
www.michiganfloral.org/education.html

■ **Louisiana State Florists' Association**
http://www.lsfaonline.com/education
/floraldesigncourses.html

■ **California State Floral Association**
www.californiacertifiedflorist.org